W9-AQV-536

Date: 5/5/16

J 945 ROB
Robinson, Joanna Jarc,
Italy /

PALM BEACH COUNTY
LIBRARY SYSTEM
3650 SUMMIT BLVD.
WEST PALM BEACH, FL 33406

ITALY

by Joanna J. Robinson

The Child's World

Published by The Child's World®
1980 Lookout Drive • Mankato, MN 56003-1705
800-599-READ • www.childsworld.com

Acknowledgments
The Child's World®: Mary Berendes, Publishing Director
Red Line Editorial: Editorial direction
The Design Lab: Design
Amnet: Production

Design elements: Claudio Divizia/iStock/Thinkstock; Shutterstock
Images
Photographs ©: Max Topchii/Shutterstock Images, cover (right);
Claudio Divizia/iStock/Thinkstock, cover (left center), 1 (bottom
left), 16 (left); Shutterstock Images, cover (left top), cover (left bottom),
1 (top), 1 (bottom right), 11, 15, 16 (right), 20, 21, 24, 25, 27,
28, 30; iStockphoto, 5; Luciano Mortula/Shutterstock Images, 6-7;
Vaclav Volrab/Shutterstock Images, 8; Matej Kastelic/Shutterstock
Images, 9; Iakov Kalinin/Shutterstock Images, 12; Claudio
Giovanni Colombo/Shutterstock Images, 17; Alex Salcedo/
iStockphoto, 19 (bottom); Marcel Clemens/Shutterstock Images, 22;
Roberto Zilli/Shutterstock Images, 23; Gianluca Figliola Fantini/
Shutterstock Images, 26

Copyright © 2016 by The Child's World®
All rights reserved. No part of this book may be
reproduced or utilized in any form or by any
means without written permission from
the publisher.

ISBN 9781634070508
LCCN 2014959743

Printed in the United States of America
Mankato, MN
July, 2015
PA02268

ABOUT THE AUTHOR

Joanna J. Robinson is a creative educational writer. She has a passion for providing fun learning materials for children of all ages. Robinson has written tons of educational content and more than 100 original stories. Trips to Mexico, Italy, England, Canada, and Egypt inspire Robinson to share her experiences with young readers.

ONE WORLD • COUNTRIES

LA TORRE DI PISA

ITALIA L.50

TABLE OF CONTENTS

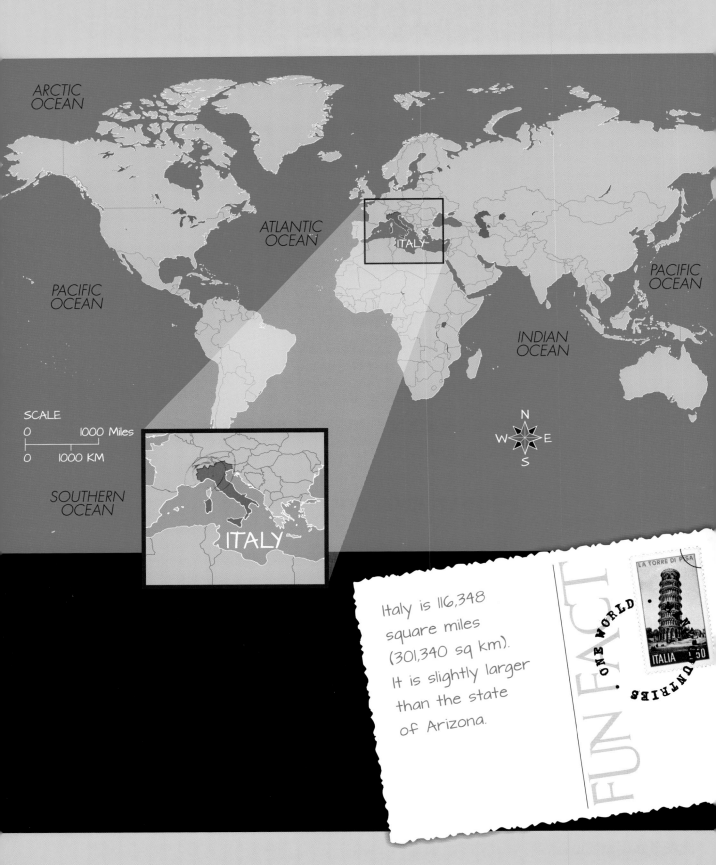

ARCTIC
OCEAN

ATLANTIC
OCEAN

ITALY

PACIFIC
OCEAN

PACIFIC
OCEAN

INDIAN
OCEAN

N
W E
S

SCALE

0   1000 Miles

0   1000 KM

SOUTHERN
OCEAN

ITALY

FUN FACT • ONE WORLD • COUNTRIES

LA TORRE DI PISA

ITALIA L.50

Italy is 116,348
square miles
(301,340 sq km).
It is slightly larger
than the state
of Arizona.

CHAPTER 1

WELCOME TO ITALY!

The morning sun sparkles off the water in the **canals** of Venice, Italy. The people of Venice are starting their day. Many head to work or school. They do not ride in cars or buses, though. They take boats!

In Venice, people take boats wherever they need to go. That is because Venice does not have roads. Instead, it has many canals. The canals are busy with *vaporetti*. They are water taxis. *Vaporetti* are a common way to travel in Venice.

A vaporetto full of passengers makes its way down the Grand Canal in Venice.

The *vaporetti* pass gondolas along the canals. Gondolas are flat, narrow boats made of wood. A gondolier drives the boat. He stands up in the back of the gondola and paddles with one oar. In ancient Venice, wealthy people rode in gondolas. Today, tourists mainly ride in gondolas.

Vaporetti and gondolas travel past shops, palaces, and churches. Riders may see Murano Island. It is famous for its art glass. Some of the boats also travel down the Grand Canal. They go under the famous Rialto Bridge.

The canals of Venice are just one part of Italy. Italy is a country with a long and proud history. It has beautiful cities with narrow, winding streets. The warm waters of the Mediterranean Sea splash on its shores. Italy also has famous cathedrals, monuments, and fountains. These beautiful structures have become symbols of Italy.

The Rialto Bridge spans the narrowest part of the Grand Canal. The bridge was built in 1591.

CHAPTER 2

THE LAND

In the spring, wildflowers grow near the Italian Alps.

Italy is in Europe. It is a **peninsula**. The peninsula is shaped a bit like a boot. Its shape gave Italy the nickname "the boot." Italy's peninsula is on the Mediterranean Sea. Italy borders Austria, France, Slovenia, and Switzerland.

Northern Italy has mountains. They are called the Italian Alps. The Alps have high, rocky peaks. Evergreens, moss, and shrubs grow along their slopes. This region of Italy is often cold. The cool weather and steep peaks make the Alps a popular place to ski.

Southern Italy is much different. This region is hot and dry. Southern Italy is often called *Mezzogiorno*, which means "midday" in Italian. It earned this name because of how strong the sun is there during the middle of the day. The Apennine Range are mountains in this part of Italy.

Italy has many cities along the sea. They are built into the mountains. The Cinque Terre is a group of five seaside cities. They form an area called the Italian Riviera. The weather there

Riomaggiore is a fishing village that is part of the Cinque Terre.

is mild and sunny. The sea views and warm weather make the Italian Riviera a popular vacation spot.

Italy also has many islands. The two largest are Sicily and Sardinia. They are in the Mediterranean Sea, off Italy's west coast. Sicily has Europe's most active volcano. It is Mount Etna.

Severe weather is common in Italy. Sometimes there are floods and landslides. In Southern Italy, earthquakes are common. In the mountains, large amounts of snow may fall down a mountainside and create an avalanche.

Italy has a variety of natural resources. People throughout the world use marble from Italy's mountains. This hard stone is made into monuments, statues, floors, and tabletops. The waters off the coastal cities are rich in fish. The land throughout Italy is good for growing grapes. In southern Italy, olive trees grow well. These crops are used to make olive oil and wine.

Italy is the second-largest producer of olive oil. About 170 million olive trees grow in Italy. The olives are pressed into oil at one of Italy's 6,000 olive mills.

FUN FACT

ONE WORLD · MANY COUNTRIES

LA TORRE DI PISA
ITALIA L.50

CHAPTER 3

GOVERNMENT AND CITIES

People went to the Colosseum to watch battles between professional fighters called gladiators. Fans also watched animal fights, athletic games, and sea battles there.

Italy's formal name is the Italian **Republic**. It has 20 regions. They are similar to states. Of the regions, 15 are regular and five are special. The regular regions govern themselves, but still have to follow the national laws. The special regions have more freedom and power to govern themselves.

Italy's national government is a republic. It has a president who serves a seven-year term. The president runs the government and commands the military. The president also appoints a prime minister. The prime minister works with lawmakers and people in government departments.

Rome is the capital of Italy. About 3.2 million people live there. Rome is located along the Tiber River in central Italy. Rome has many historic buildings. The Pantheon is a temple for ancient Roman gods. The Colosseum is one of the first arenas. These buildings are nearly 2,000 years old. They are still standing today.

Rome is also home to Vatican City. It governs itself separately from the rest of Italy. Vatican City is where the Pope lives. He is the leader of the Roman Catholic Church. People from all over the world travel to Vatican City to hear him speak.

Milan is another large Italian city. It is the heart of fashion. Stores there sell Italian brands, such as Versace and Gucci. These brands are also sold all over the world. The city of Pisa is home to the leaning tower. This tall bell tower leans to the side. It is a popular place for tourists to visit. The city of Pompeii has ruins from Vesuvius. This volcano erupted and buried the town with hot lava and ash in 79 AD.

The city of Florence was the birthplace of the Italian **Renaissance**. This was an important period of time. It lasted from the 1300s to the 1500s. During this time, people made great discoveries in art, science, and math.

Brunelleschi designed the dome for the Cathedral of Santa Maria del Fiore in Florence.

Works made during the Renaissance are familiar to people across the globe. During this time, the artist Leonardo da Vinci created the *Mona Lisa*. Michelangelo sculpted *David* and painted **frescoes** on the ceiling of the Sistine Chapel in Vatican City. Filippo Brunelleschi created the first dome for a church in Florence. Today buildings all over the world have Italian features, such as the dome.

Italy is also known across the world for the goods it **exports**. The goods include sports cars, designer clothing, and leather shoes. Italy is also known for its wine. It is one of the world's largest wine producers. Each region in Italy has a special wine. Italian wine is sold across the world.

Italian currency

Italian flag

Grapes grow on farms called vineyards, such as this one in Florence. The grapes grown on vineyards are made into wine.

GLOBAL CONNECTIONS

When it comes to trade, one of the best things about Italy is its location. Italy is in the middle of many seas. It is close to many countries. This makes trading easier. Italy trades with countries in Europe, North Africa, and the Middle East. Other trading partners include the United States, Russia, and China.

These places welcome Italian goods. People in other countries want the latest fashions from Italian designers. They want to drive fast Italian cars. They want real Italian food and wine. The goods from Italy are high quality and in demand.

Italy is part of the European Union (EU). This group is made up of 28 European countries. They share resources and work together. They try to solve problems in Europe, such as crime and drug use.

The EU makes life easier for its residents, too. People can move between countries freely. They can work, study, live, and get married in nearby countries. Residents can buy and sell easily in other countries. That's because most Union countries use the same money, the euro.

Italy **imports** many goods, too. Most of Italy's coal comes from Russia, South Africa, the United States, and China. Italy uses coal for electricity and energy. Other imports include chemicals, machines, and metals. Italy imports clothes, food, beverages, and tobacco, too.

FUN FACT

The sign for the euro looks like a capital letter "E" with two lines through it, €. The "E" stands for Europe, and the two lines show that the money is stable and strong.

LA TORRE DI PISA

ONE WORLD

COUNTRIES

ITALIA L.50

PIZZA MARGHERITA E BIBITA
€3,50

PIZZA FARCITA E BIBITA
€ 4,00

PANINI CON SALUMI €3,50
O FORMAGGI

BUON APPETITO!!

CHAPTER 4

PEOPLE AND CULTURES

A family enjoys pizza in an outdoor café in Rome. Family meals are an important part of life in Italy.

Life in Italy centers around food and family. Families enjoy meals together. Favorite foods include pastries, rice, fish, and citrus fruit. Pasta is also popular. In the South, people like pasta with sauce. They use olive oil, tomatoes, and spices. In the North, people like pasta with cream, butter, and cheese.

During Epiphany celebrations, children hear stories about La Befana. She is a witch who brings children presents as she looks for baby Jesus.

In Italy, most people speak Italian. Most Italians follow the Roman Catholic religion. They celebrate religious holidays such as Carnevale. This holiday takes place right before **Lent**. People celebrate with food, parties, shows, and music. They also wear masks and have parades.

On January 6, Italians celebrate Epiphany. Catholics believe this is when the three wise men visited Jesus. Religious festivities are common. There are parades. People dress in historical costumes. There are races down the canal in Venice.

Italians also celebrate national holidays. **Liberation** Day is celebrated on April 25. It marks Italy's freedom from Germany after World War II (1939–1945). Italians remember the people who fought in the war. They have concerts and food festivals. There are public activities such as rallies and gatherings.

Italy celebrates its government, too. Republic Day is on June 2. People remember when Italy became a republic in 1946. They celebrate with parades and ceremonies.

FUN FACT

Italians make some of the world's fastest cars. Their carmakers include Ferrari, Maserati, and Lamborghini. Italy's state police use Lamborghinis as their police cars. The cars have the word *polizia* painted on the side. The cars come with special police equipment, such as radars and flashing lights.

ONE WORLD • MANY COUNTRIES

LA TORRE DI PISA
ITALIA L.50

Military leaders raise the Italian flag during a ceremony in the city of Turin for Republic Day.

CHAPTER 5

DAILY LIFE

↖ Many Italians enjoy spending their free time outdoors. These Italian children wear special helmets to explore one of Italy's many caves.

Italians enjoy many daily activities. They watch television and listen to the radio. They read newspapers and go to the movies. Young Italians meet with their friends. They go to pizzerias and dance clubs.

Many Italians work for small companies. Some work for family businesses. During the workday, many Italians take a two-hour lunch break.

Each part of Italy has special foods. In the North, dishes often include butter, rice, polenta, and cheeses. On the coast, Italians enjoy seafood. Central Italy has meat dishes, such as wild boar. Southern Italy has citrus fruits, olives, and different kinds of wine.

Family-run fish stands are common at outdoor markets in Italy, such as this one in Venice.

Pizza is a favorite Italian food. There are two kinds of pizza. One has a thick crust. The other has a thin crust. Italians use wheat flour to make the dough. Pizza is cooked in a brick oven. Spinach and cheese are common toppings.

For dessert, Italians enjoy pastries and other sweets. Tiramisu is a sponge cake with mascarpone cheese. Cannolis are cookies with a cheesy filling and pistachio nuts. Gelato is a popular frozen treat in many parts of Italy, too. Many Italians also enjoy cappuccino. It is a special coffee drink with hot milk.

Gelato is a soft, rich ice cream. It comes in flavors like chocolate, pistachio, or vanilla.

Famous fashion designers live and work in Italy. Many Italians like to follow fashion closely. In Italy, fashion is more than just clothes. It is a way of life. It is how Italians present themselves to the world. Italian clothing is well made. People often like to wear finely tailored clothes.

Parmesan cheese is from Parma, Italy. Italians also make other cheeses, such as gorgonzola, mozzarella, provolone, and ricotta.

FUN FACT

ONE WORLD · COUNTRIES

LA TORRE DI PISA

ITALIA L.50

Italians have many ways to get from place to place. In cities, people drive cars and motorcycles. They can also ride bicycles, buses, and trains. Rome, Milan, and Naples have subways. Ferries carry people from the mainland to the islands of Sicily and Sardinia.

From its sunny islands to its snowy mountains, Italy is a beautiful country. For centuries, Italians have created buildings, art, food, and fashion that the world admires. Today, Italians honor their past while creating a modern nation that is unlike any other.

Italians ride bicycles to get from place to place. They also ride bicycles for fun.

DAILY LIFE FOR CHILDREN

Children are special to Italian families. They represent the future. All children attend school. School begins at 8:00 in the morning. It ends at 1:00 in the afternoon.

In school, students learn Italian and English. They learn geography, history, math, science, and technology. They also study music, art, physical education, and religion. Students must memorize facts and follow rules.

In the afternoon, children eat lunch and take a nap or rest. They do their homework. They might practice or play sports. At night, children use the computer or watch television. They talk to friends, read, or listen to music. They eat a late dinner and then go to bed soon after.

FAST FACTS

Population: 61 million

Area: 116,348 square miles (301,340 sq km)

Capital: Rome

Largest Cities: Rome, Milan, and Naples

Form of Government: Republic

Language: Italian

Trading Partners:
Germany, France, and
the United States

Major Holidays:
Liberation Day, Republic
Day, Christmas, Epiphany,
Carnevale, and Easter

National Dishes:
Pizza, Pasta, Polenta, Gelato

A gondolier makes his way
down a quiet canal in Venice.

GLOSSARY

canals (cah-NALs) Canals are long, narrow waterways created by people for boats. Gondolas travel down the canals in Venice.

exports (ek-SPORTs) Exports are goods sold to another country. Italy exports many products to other countries.

frescoes (FRES-cos) Frescoes are paintings that are made in fresh plaster. Michelangelo is famous for his frescoes.

imports (ihm-PORTs) Imports are goods brought into another country to trade or sell. Italy imports many goods.

Lent (LEHNT) Lent is the 40 weekdays before Easter. Italians celebrate Carnevale before Lent begins.

liberation (lib-uh-RAY-shun) Liberation is the act of freeing a person from another's control. Italy celebrates Liberation Day each year.

peninsula (puh-NIN-suh-luh) A peninsula is a landform that is almost completely surrounded by water. Italy is a peninsula.

Renaissance (REN-uh-sahnss) The Renaissance was a period of art, learning, and discovery in Europe during the 14th and 16th centuries. Many scientific discoveries were made during the Italian Renaissance.

republic (ri-PUHB-lik) A republic is a form of government in which people elect their leaders. Italy is a republic.

TO LEARN MORE

BOOKS

Borlenghi, Patricia. *Find Out About Italy*. Hauppauge, NY: Barron's Educational Series, 2006.

Family Guide: Italy. New York: Dorling Kindersley, 2012.

Sasek, Miroslav. *This is Rome*. New York: Universe, 2007.

WEB SITES

Visit our Web site for links about Italy: **childsworld.com/links**

Note to Parents, Teachers, and Librarians: We routinely verify our Web links to make sure they are safe and active sites. So encourage your readers to check them out!

INDEX